JOANN NEISH METZ

O9-CFT-495

JOANN NEISH METZ

O9-CFT-495

ORIGINAL ART DECO DESIGNS

72 PLATES
BY
WILLIAM ROWE

DOVER PUBLICATIONS, INC.
NEW YORK

Copyright © 1973 by Dover Publications, Inc.
All rights reserved under Pan American and International Copyright Conventions.

Published in Canada by General Publishing Company, Ltd., 30 Lesmill Road, Don Mills, Toronto, Ontario.
Published in the United Kingdom by Constable and Company, Ltd., 10 Orange Street, London WC 2.

ORIGINAL ART DECO DESIGNS BY William Rowe is a new work, first published by Dover Publications, Inc., in 1973.

DOVER *Pictorial Archive* SERIES

This book belongs to the Dover Pictorial Archive Series. You may use the designs and illustrations for graphics and crafts applications, free and without special permission, provided that you include no more than ten in the same publication or project. (For permission for additional use, please write to Dover Publications, Inc., 31 East 2nd Street, Mineola, N.Y. 11501.)

However, republication or reproduction of any illustration by any other graphic service whether it be in a book or in any other design resource is strictly prohibited.

International Standard Book Number: 0-486-22567-4
Library of Congress Catalog Card Number: 73-75281

Manufactured in the United States of America
Dover Publications, Inc.
31 East 2nd Street
Mineola, N.Y. 11501

PUBLISHER'S NOTE

ART DECO, in its extended connotation as the international decorative style of the late 20's, the 30's and the early 40's, includes elements of evolved Art Nouveau, of Bauhaus, De Stijl and other vital twentieth-century trends. Its current revival has become a triumphal procession, joined by many young designers who were not yet born when the style originally flourished.

William Rowe, a young artist of unusual intelligence and taste, presents herewith his own contemporary reinterpretation of the style. Much serious research and much love and empathy are apparent in the results he has achieved. His book contains a profusion of design elements that will offer a welcome stimulus to art directors and advertisers, typographers and book designers, package designers, illustrators—even interior designers and decorators.

There are scores of geometrical borders, frames, corners, friezes and large overall patterns. On many pages of the book these elements are arranged in a way that reveals subtle interrelationships—they become almost infinitely divisible and recombinable. Often, what seems at first glance to be just one design breaks down into an amazing multiplicity of possibilities.

There is a fascinating series of numerals, which first appears on several pages as one 1, two 2's, three 3's . . . and is then summarized with variations of shading and detail.

There are seven irresistible complete alphabets, presented by the artist with his customary wit: in each case, some of the letters form the title of an outstanding popular song of the period, and the remaining letters appear in alphabetical order below. This use of song titles provides more than just fun—it shows how the letter designer himself envisions the spacing of his letters in a wide variety of word situations. And note also the pages facing the alphabets, with their visual echoes of the song titles!

The wealth of ideas also includes floral ornaments, bits of musical notation, a design for a title page and a generous helping of figurative art, culminating in a series that glorifies the material pillars of the American way of life—the toothpaste tube, the TV set, the washstand, the drinking fountain, the ice cream cone, and others.

All too seldom in the past has the work of important designers been collected in book form, and generally not until long after the artist originally made his contribution. Today, when the old distinction between "fine" and "applied" art is waning and variations on an abstract design are appreciated in the same way as variations on a still life or a genre theme, the publisher is glad to present a young man's new work in design —work in which the technical proficiency that bespeaks true dedication is combined with exceptional wit and inventiveness.

CARIOCA·LOUNGE·WEST
WALL·AND·ENTRY·STAIR

3

7

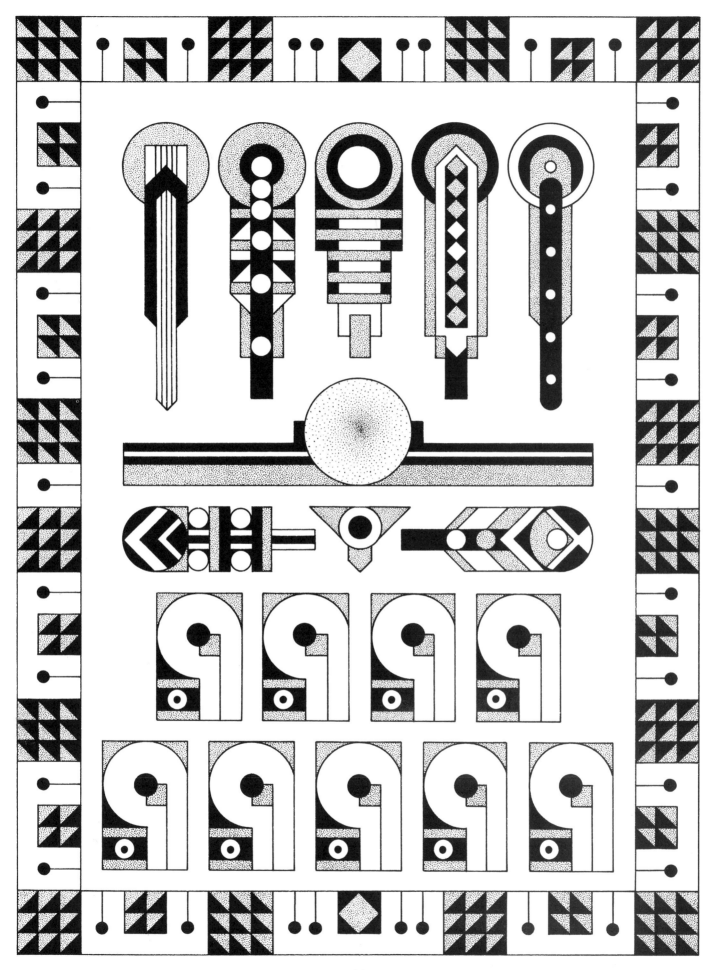

11

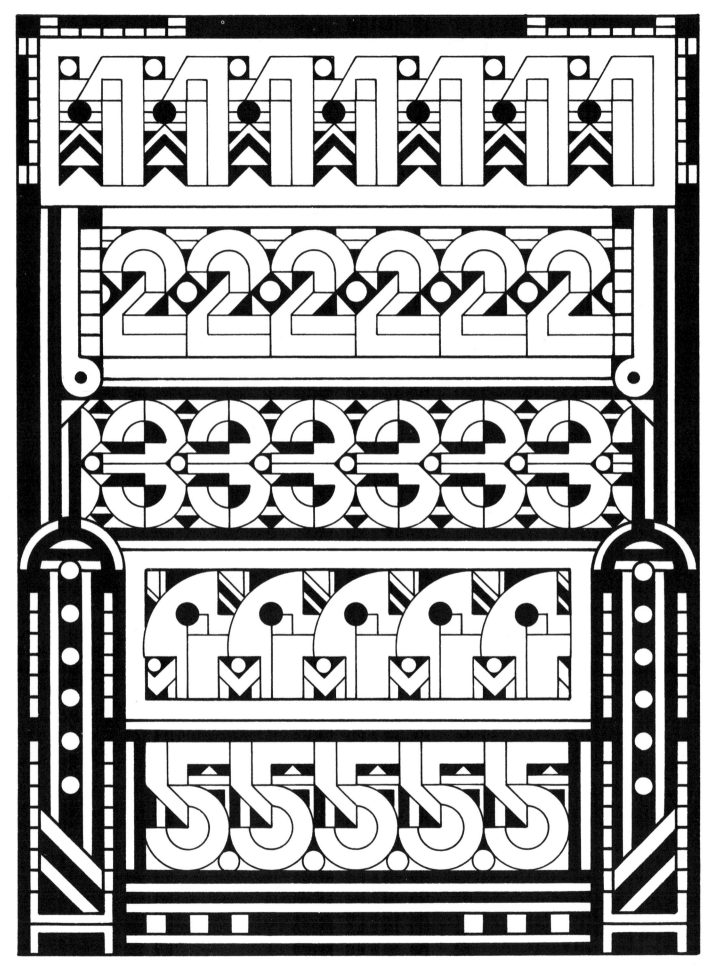

15

17

22

23

24

25

26

32

OLD FOLKS' SHUFFLE

ABCGIJM NPQRTV WXYZ

34

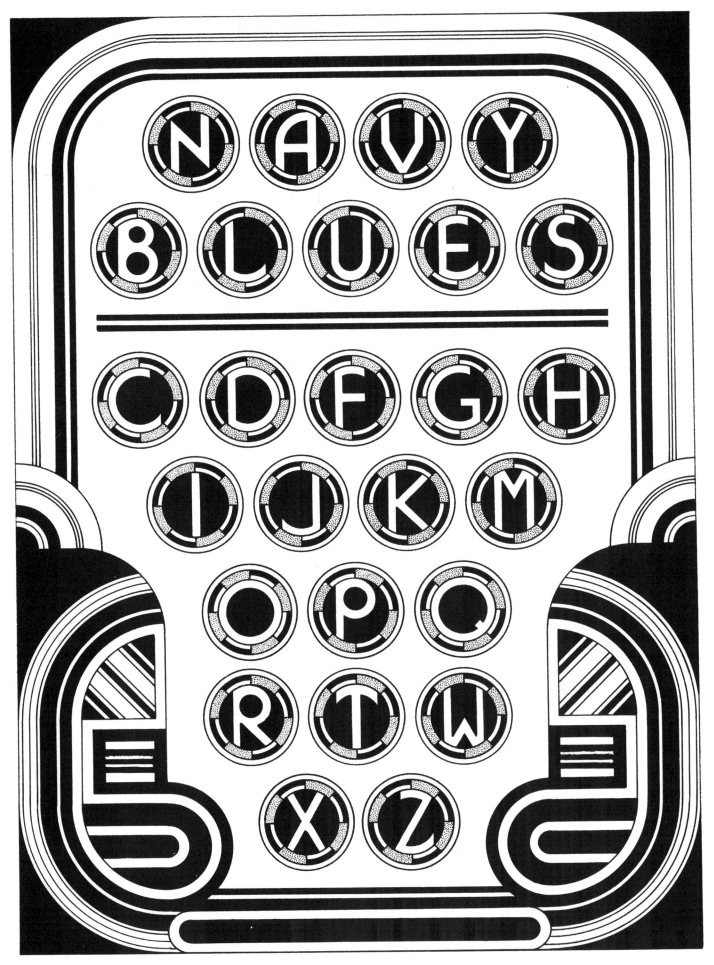

SUGAR
FOOT
STRUT

ABCDEFGH
IJKLM
NPQUV
WXYZ

40

HEEBIE
JEEBIES

ACDFG
KLMNO
PQRTU
VWXYZ

42

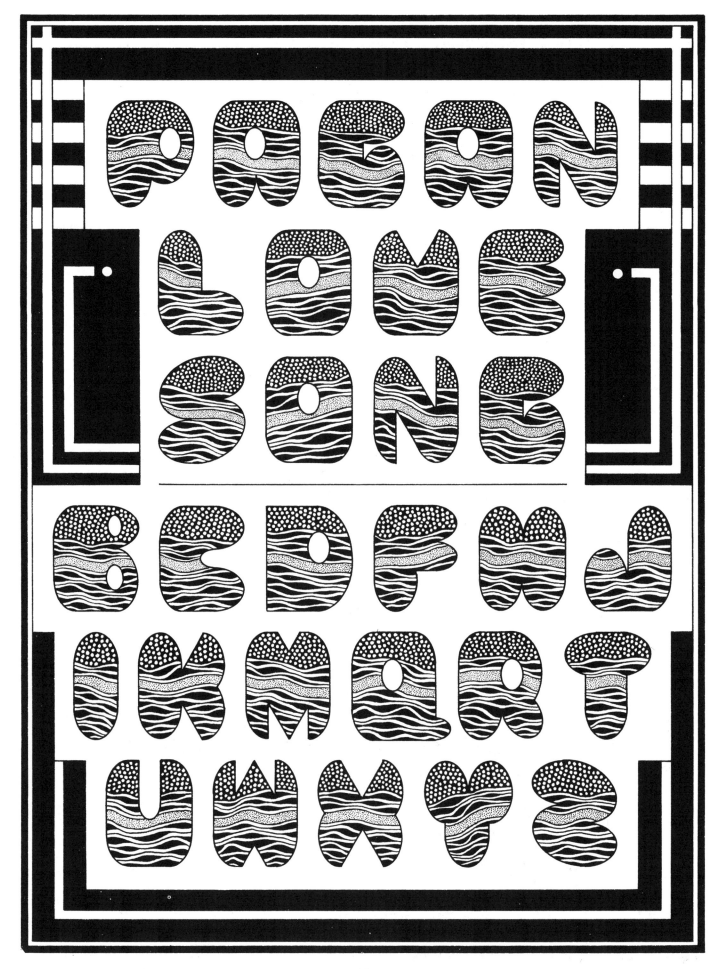

THREE
BLIND
MICE

AFGJK
OPQSU
VWXYZ

47

49

51

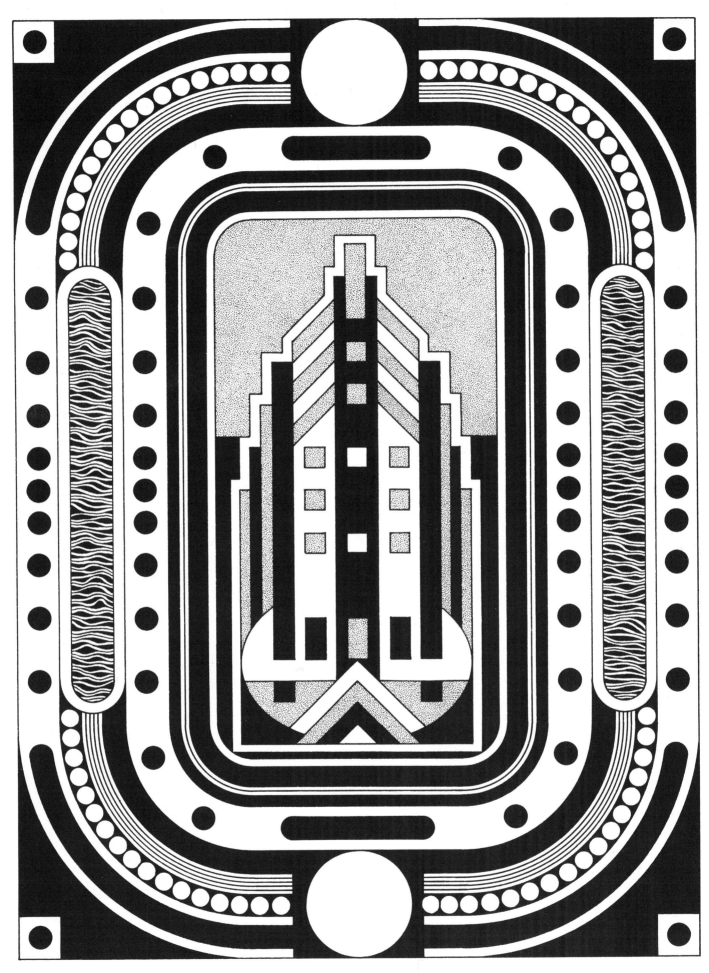

53

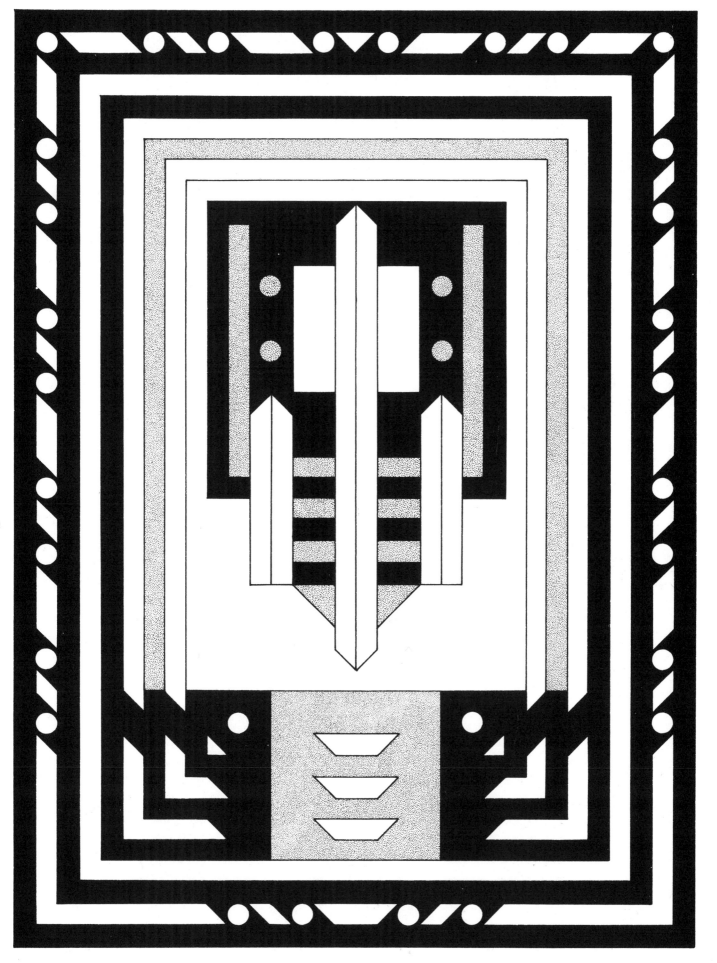

57

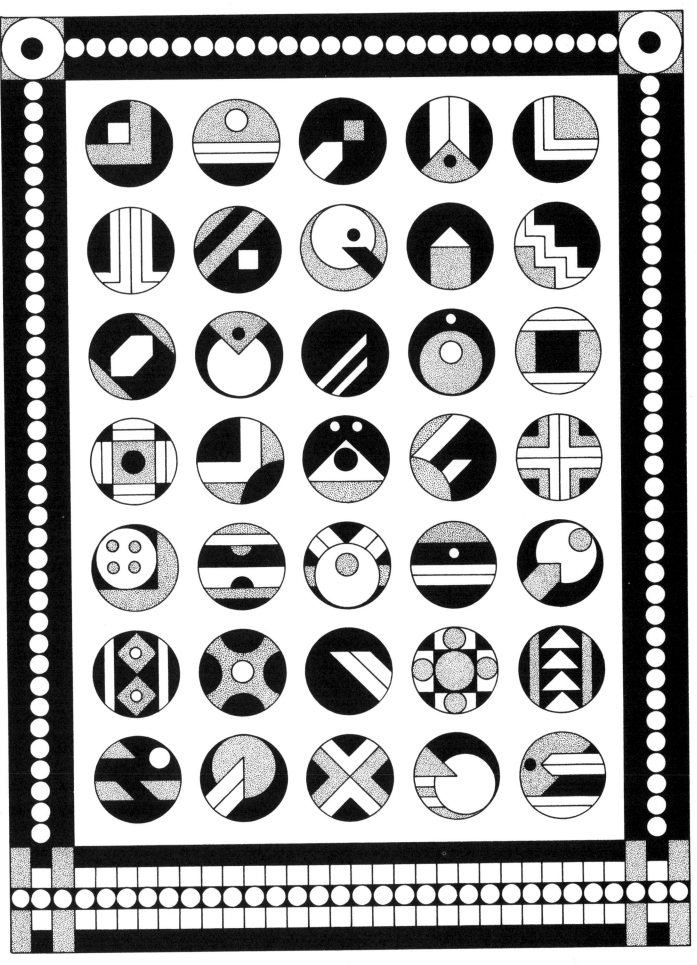

63

64

68

69

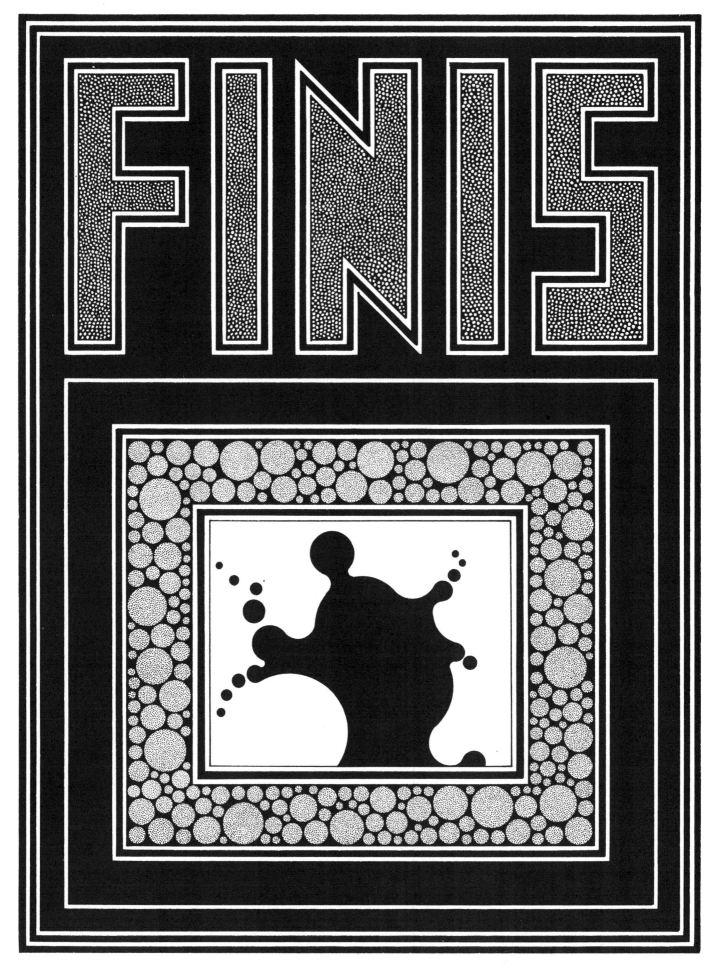